This book is dedicated to children
who are lost and alone and to those
who help them.

WALKER BOOKS
AND SUBSIDIARIES
LONDON • BOSTON • SYDNEY • AUCKLAND

Nicola Davies

illustrated by Rebecca Cobb

THE DAY WAR CAME there were flowers on the window sill and my father sang my baby brother back to sleep.

My mother made my breakfast, kissed my nose and walked with me to school.

That morning I learned about volcanoes.
I sang a song about how tadpoles
turn at last to frogs.
I drew a picture of a bird.

Then, just after lunch, war came.

At first, just like a spattering of hail,

a voice of thunder …

then all smoke and fire and noise that I didn't understand.

It came across the playground.

It came into my teacher's face.

It brought the roof down

and turned my town to rubble.

I can't say the words that tell you
about the blackened hole
that had been my home.

All I can say is this:

war took everything,

war took everyone.

I was ragged, bloody, all alone.

I ran. Walked over fields and roads and mountains

in the cold and mud and rain;

rode on the back of trucks, in buses;

went on a boat that leaked and almost sank;

then up a beach where shoes lay empty in the sand.

I ran until I couldn't run,
until I reached a row of huts
and found a corner with a dirty blanket
and a door that rattled in the wind.

But war had followed me.

It was underneath my skin,

behind my eyes,

and in my dreams.

It had taken possession of my heart.

I walked and walked to try to drive war out of myself,

to try to find a place it hadn't reached.

But war was in the way that doors shut when I came down the street.

It was in the way the people didn't smile, and turned away.

I came to a school.

I looked in through the window.

They were learning all about volcanoes,

singing and drawing birds.

I went inside.

My footsteps echoed in the hall.

I pushed the door and faces turned

towards me but the teacher didn't smile.

She said, "There is no room for you,

you see. There is no chair for you to sit on.

You have to go away."

And then I understood that

war had got here too.

I turned around and went back to the hut, the corner
and the blanket, and crawled inside.

It seemed that war had taken all the world
and all the people in it.

The door banged. I thought it was the wind – but a child's voice spoke.

"I brought you this," he said, "so you can come to school."

It was a chair.

A chair for me to sit on and learn about volcanoes, sing and draw birds.

And drive the war out of my heart.

He smiled and said, "My friends have brought theirs too,

so all the children here can come to school."

Out of every hut a child came
and we walked together,
on a road all lined with chairs.

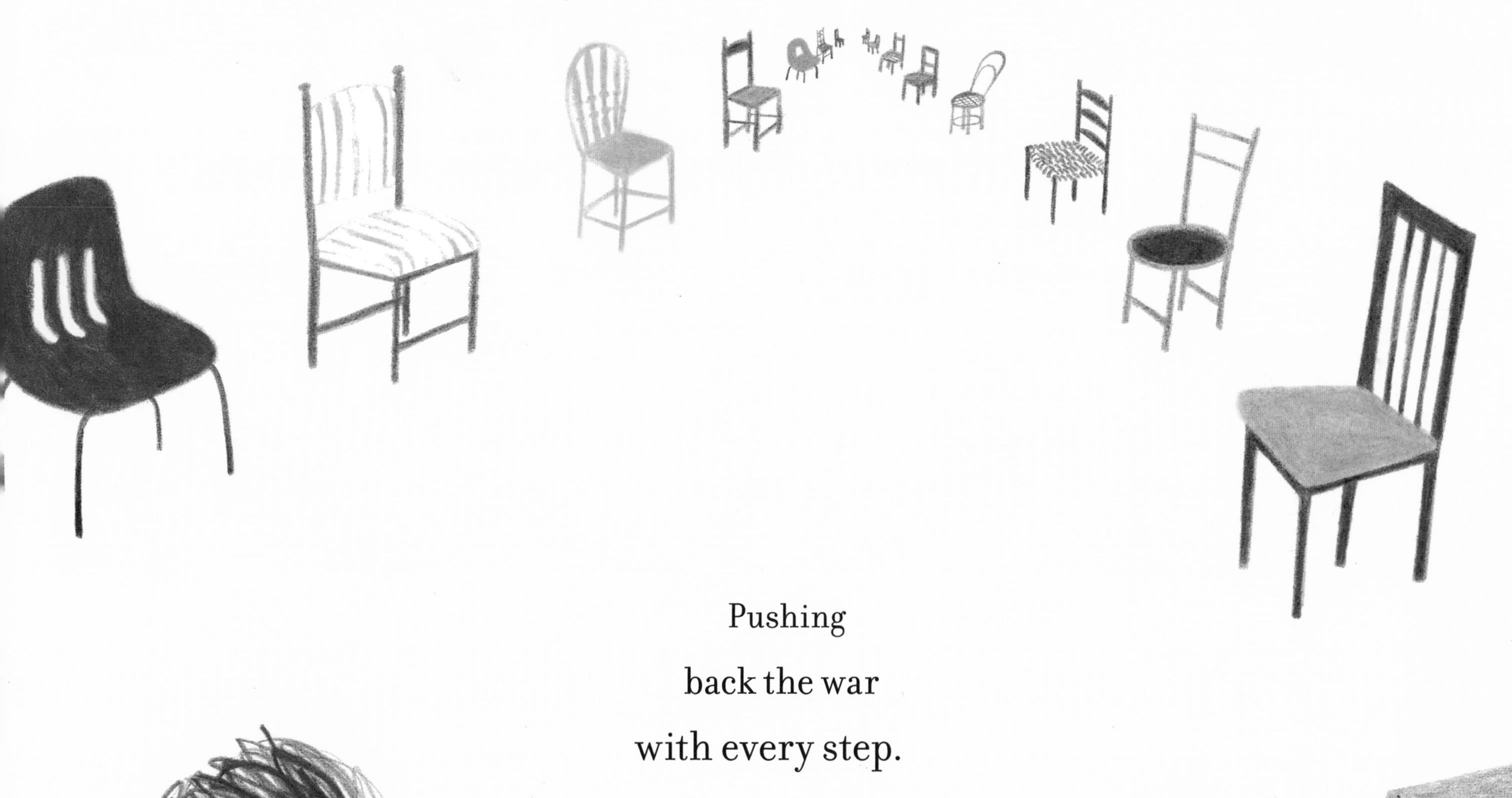

Pushing
back the war
with every step.

In the spring of 2016 the UK government refused to give sanctuary to 3,000 unaccompanied child refugees. At about the same time I heard a story about a refugee child being refused entry to a school because there wasn't a chair for her to sit on. Out of that, this poem came and was published first on the *Guardian* newspaper's website, with images of an empty chair by the artists Jackie Morris and Petr Horáček. In the days that followed, hundreds and hundreds of people posted images of empty chairs as symbols of solidarity with those children who had lost everything and had nowhere to go – and no chance of an education. I want this story to remind us all about the power of kindness and its ability to give hope for a better future.

One way you can help children like the little girl in this story is to support charities such as **Help Refugees**. Founded by a group of friends who saw the worsening situation for refugees in Europe and wanted to do something about it, Help Refugees now supports over 70 projects to aid refugees worldwide with funding, food, shelter and volunteers. Filling gaps left by governments and large NGOs, they respond to the genuine needs of refugees and displaced populations in a fast, flexible and empowering way. Go to **helprefugees.org** to learn more about their work and how you can help.

Nicola Davies

First published 2018 by Walker Books Ltd, 87 Vauxhall Walk, London SE11 5HJ

This edition published 2019

2 4 6 8 10 9 7 5 3 1

This book has been typeset in Filosofia OT

Printed in China

British Library Cataloguing in Publication Data: a catalogue record for this book is available from the British Library

ISBN 978-1-4063-8293-8

www.walker.co.uk